C000015573

Threads of Gold

Words to
encourage and inspire

Catherine Aldis

**kevin
mayhew**

First published in 2002 by
KEVIN MAYHEW LTD
Buxhall, Stowmarket
Suffolk IP14 3BW
Email: info@kevinmayhewltd.com

0 1 2 3 4 5 6 7 8 9

ISBN 1 84003 923 X
Catalogue No. 1500515

Illustrated by Angela Palfrey
Printed and bound in China

Contents

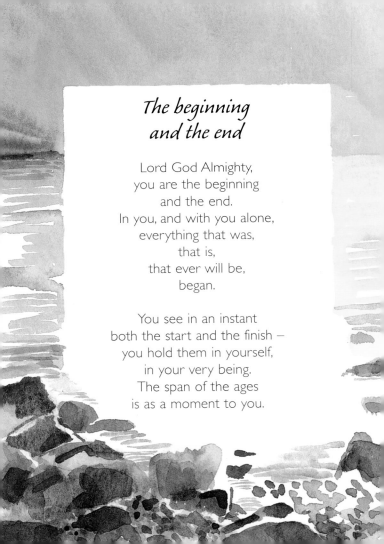

The beginning
and the end

Lord God Almighty,
you are the beginning
and the end.
In you, and with you alone,
everything that was,
that is,
that ever will be,
began.

You see in an instant
both the start and the finish –
you hold them in yourself,
in your very being.
The span of the ages
is as a moment to you.

4

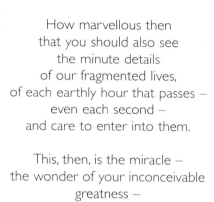

How marvellous then
that you should also see
the minute details
of our fragmented lives,
of each earthly hour that passes –
even each second –
and care to enter into them.

This, then, is the miracle –
the wonder of your inconceivable
greatness –
stooping to enter
our earthbound smallness,
and by your entry
transforming the finite to infinite,
and drawing humanity
towards eternity.

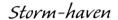

Storm-haven

You know me through and through
and so I give myself to you.
You are the one safe place,
the only haven from the storm –
there is no other.
In you I hide,
my Shelter and my Comforter.
Forgive the things
which keep me from your side,
which hold me back,
that I may enter in
between the harbour walls
to anchor deeply,
rest untossed,
and find your peace at last.

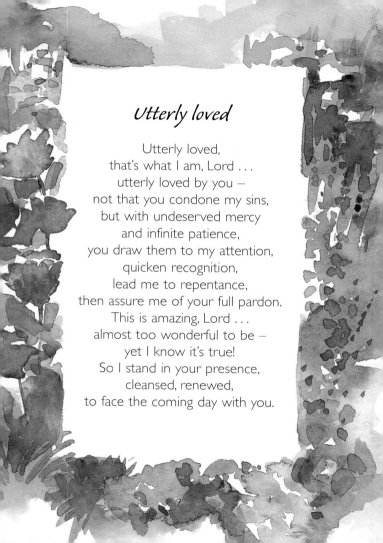

Utterly loved

Utterly loved,
that's what I am, Lord . . .
utterly loved by you –
not that you condone my sins,
but with undeserved mercy
and infinite patience,
you draw them to my attention,
quicken recognition,
lead me to repentance,
then assure me of your full pardon.
This is amazing, Lord . . .
almost too wonderful to be –
yet I know it's true!
So I stand in your presence,
cleansed, renewed,
to face the coming day with you.

I know there is a time

I know there is a time
for building, Lord,
for extending boundaries,
for marching out in faith
to claim the land.
I also know there is a time
for standing still,
for waiting quietly,
watching, praying,
allowing trust and hope
to be renewed.

Oh Lord, please teach me
which is which.

Leaving behind
the past

Leaving behind the past,
the yesterdays of my life,
the puzzles and pains
of what is now history,
I turn afresh to you,
the God of new beginnings,
and put my hand once more
into yours.

Drawing aside the curtain
on to the gift of today,
I take a step, as it were,
into the unknown –
unknown, that is, to me,
but not to you.
So I let this thought
take hold in me
and reassure my heart:
I need not be afraid
for it is enough to know
that you see the future –
and I see you.

Your perfect timing

I will wait for you, Lord,
to work out your purposes
in my life.
Let me sense your controlling hand
and rest in the knowledge
of your master-plan,
perfect in its shape and form.
Let me glimpse
the beauty of your designs,
and rejoice in the turning
of each new page,
the unfolding of every part.

Let me appreciate your perfect timing,
neither rebelling nor questioning
when your purposes are hidden,
but waiting quietly
for your meaning to illuminate
my circumstances.

Not in my own strength, Lord,
can I do this,
but only by your grace
at work in my life –
until your re-creation
is finally perfected in me.

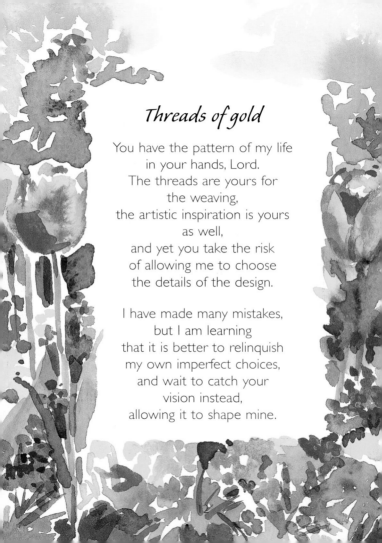

Threads of gold

You have the pattern of my life
in your hands, Lord.
The threads are yours for
the weaving,
the artistic inspiration is yours
as well,
and yet you take the risk
of allowing me to choose
the details of the design.

I have made many mistakes,
but I am learning
that it is better to relinquish
my own imperfect choices,
and wait to catch your
vision instead,
allowing it to shape mine.

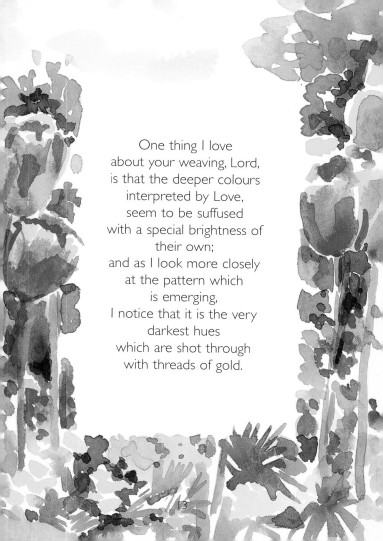

One thing I love
about your weaving, Lord,
is that the deeper colours
interpreted by Love,
seem to be suffused
with a special brightness of
their own;
and as I look more closely
at the pattern which
is emerging,
I notice that it is the very
darkest hues
which are shot through
with threads of gold.

Moments

From before the birth of time,
the conception of hours and days,
throughout all history, known, unknown,
the pattern of all our ways,
you have been God,
your sovereignty secure,
and you will still be God
tomorrow
and for evermore.

So what if all you call me to,
is this:
to let you be God
in this particular moment,
this circumstance, this day?
Then, Lord,
I choose to leave the past behind,
and when I pray,
thrust all thoughts of the future
firmly into your hands –
and I ask you, Lord,
to help me live
in moments.

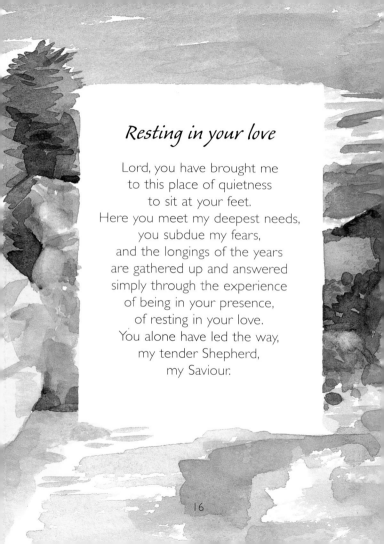

Resting in your love

Lord, you have brought me
to this place of quietness
to sit at your feet.
Here you meet my deepest needs,
you subdue my fears,
and the longings of the years
are gathered up and answered
simply through the experience
of being in your presence,
of resting in your love.
You alone have led the way,
my tender Shepherd,
my Saviour.

Oh let me not rush on from here
too quickly.
Forbid it, Lord,
that I should look ahead
too soon,
lest I should miss a moment
of your blessing
and instead of leaning on
your strength,
should go out in my own.

Cords of love

In all the small turnings-away
from you, Lord,
I gradually distance myself
from the experience
of your indwelling presence,
until close communion with you
is merely a memory.

When that happens, Lord,
please draw me back
with cords of love
from your father-heart,
and when I have seen again
the extent of your love for me,
help me to submit myself
once more to you,
and return
to that special place of rest
which is your gift to me.

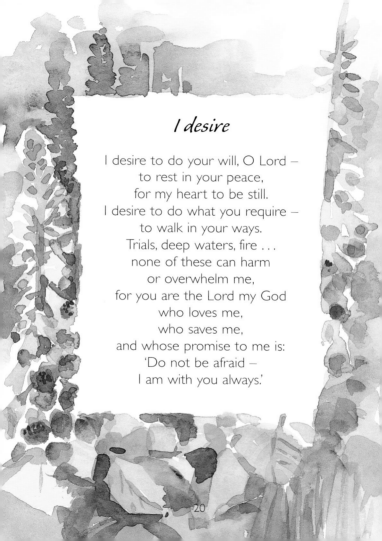

I desire

I desire to do your will, O Lord –
to rest in your peace,
for my heart to be still.
I desire to do what you require –
to walk in your ways.
Trials, deep waters, fire . . .
none of these can harm
or overwhelm me,
for you are the Lord my God
who loves me,
who saves me,
and whose promise to me is:
'Do not be afraid –
I am with you always.'

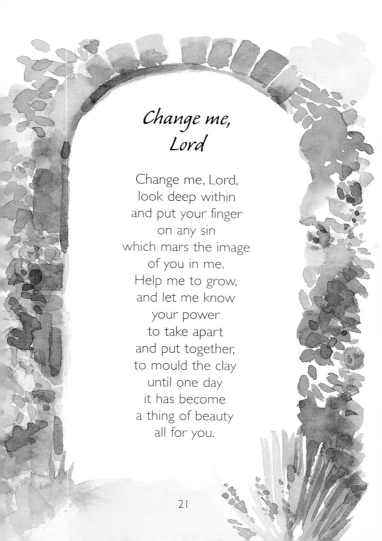

Change me,
Lord

Change me, Lord,
look deep within
and put your finger
on any sin
which mars the image
of you in me.
Help me to grow,
and let me know
your power
to take apart
and put together,
to mould the clay
until one day
it has become
a thing of beauty
all for you.

I bow before you

I bow before you, King of heaven,
most glorious Majesty
and deepest, richest Love.
At your throne I kneel
with empty hands
for all I have to offer you
are shattered dreams
and broken plans.

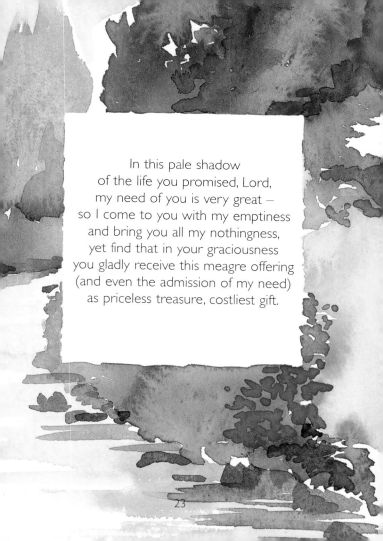

In this pale shadow
of the life you promised, Lord,
my need of you is very great —
so I come to you with my emptiness
and bring you all my nothingness,
yet find that in your graciousness
you gladly receive this meagre offering
(and even the admission of my need)
as priceless treasure, costliest gift.

Snowflakes

Sometimes, Lord,
I lose sight of you,
then somehow, Lord,
I can't find my way through
the muddles and messes
of my life —
pride, misunderstandings,
thoughtless words . . .
they all mount up, Lord,
until suddenly I'm trapped
in a web of my own weaving.

I cry out to you for help,
confessing my need of you –
then slowly,
almost imperceptibly,
like snowflakes gently descending
one by one,
quietly covering the earth,
so your stillness settles
in my heart,
and everything else falls away,
taking its proper place
in relation to you.

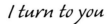

I turn to you

I turn to you, God of the universe,
creator of heaven and earth.
You are my God
and I belong to you.

I turn to you, Father of all life
from the beginning of time.
You are my Father
and I am your child.

I turn to you, King of the nations –
under your rule come justice and peace.
You are my King
and I submit my life to you.

I turn to you, Saviour of the world,
whose blood cleanses away all sin.
You are my Saviour
and you have redeemed me.

I turn to you, O Great Healer –
you speak the word and it is done.
You are my Healer
and I await your touch.

I turn to you, life-giving Spirit,
who breathes God's presence into
my heart.
You are my Sustainer
and I ask you to fill me again.

The well of your love

When pain overwhelms me, Lord,
and I struggle to believe
your promises,
let me sink deeply
into the well of your love,
and know your great compassion.

When self-pity threatens to
engulf me, Lord,
and I drown in my own sorrows,
let me sink deeply
into the well of your love,
and see also the sufferings of others.

When despair lurks round the
corner, Lord,
and all my hopes are dashed away,
let me sink deeply
into the well of your love,
and be bathed in your peace.

When fear paralyses me, Lord,
and terror presses me down
into an abyss,
let me sink deeply
into the well of your love,
and experience your power to save.

When doubts attack me, Lord,
and the very ground I stand upon
appears to shift,
let me sink deeply
into the well of your love,
and there find you.

Hope of the ages

Hope of the ages,
year upon year
your people waited,
believing,
yet not understanding
the object of their longing.

The Light dawned,
shone in the darkness –
but that Light was misunderstood,
even scorned by many,
recognised
and welcomed with great joy
by only a few.

Hope of the world,
we too await your coming.
Our hearts are longing
for the Son of Righteousness
to appear.

Hope of our lives,
let us not hope in vain things,
but let all our yearning
be rooted and centred
in you.

Deeper into you

Enfolded in your peace,
leaning on your goodness,
resting in your arms,
surrounded by your love,
tenderly laid on your shoulder,
lifted by strong hands,
gently led forward
along your way –
through sorrow to joy,
darkness to light,
night to day,
from fear to freedom,
doubt to faith,
storm to calm,
turmoil to peace,
through life . . .
to Life –
deeper into you.